The Ramayana

An imprint of Om Books International

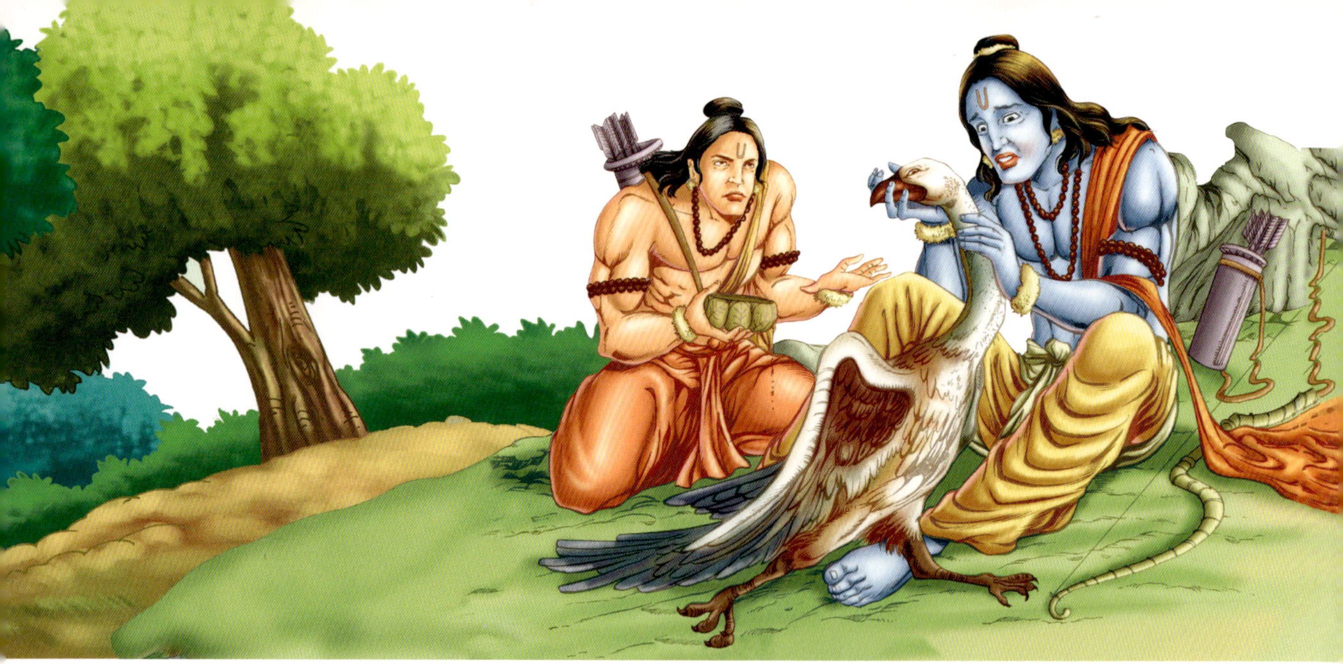

First publihsed in 2022 by

Om KIDZ | Om Books International

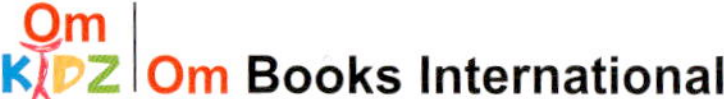

Corporate & Editorial Office
A-12, Sector 64, Noida 201 301
Uttar Pradesh, India
Phone: +91 120 477 4100
Email: editorial@ombooks.com
Website: www.ombooksinternational.com

Sales Office
107, Ansari Road, Darya Ganj
New Delhi 110 002, India
Phone: +91 11 4000 9000
Email: sales@ombooks.com

Retold by Kirti Pathak
Design: Harish Arya

ISBN: 978-93-84225-04-9

Printed in China

10 9 8 7 6 5 4 3 2 1

Contents

Rama's Illustrious Childhood

Thousands of years ago, Ayodhya was ruled by the noble King Dashratha of the Solar Dynasty (Surya Vansha). He had three beautiful and virtuous queens. There was great bonding between them. However, a shadow of gloom was always present in their hearts because they did not have any children.

King Dashratha performed a yajna as advised by Sage Vashistha, the royal priest. Out of the yajna fire, a divine figure emerged with a bowl of prasad for the queens. In due course, the queens gave birth to four divine sons - Rama (the incarnation of Lord Vishnu) was born to the eldest queen Kaushalya, Bharata to Kaikeyi and the twins Lakshmana and Shatrughna were born to the youngest queen, Sumitra.

There was much celebration throughout Ayodhya. The crowds sang, danced and played on various musical instruments. Rich gifts were distributed among the people. The gods blessed and showered flowers from above.

Joy and prosperity reigned in all the worlds of Heaven, Earth and beyond.

It was an auspicious moment for which the Universe had been waiting.

The king and the queens enjoyed the innocent mischief of the four little princes who were loved by all. They were obedient, gentle and well-behaved. The people of Ayodhya were very fond of them.

Rama in particular was so charming that whoever saw him was hypnotised by his magnetic attraction.

As the princes grew, they were sent to Sage Vashishtha's Ashram. There they mastered the Vedas. They also learnt to ride horses and elephants, drive chariots and hunt in the forests. They were trained to become skilful warriors. Their accuracy in shooting arrows to hit the desired target filled their father's heart with great pride.

The princes also imbibed the virtues of humility and discipline.

All the brothers were devoted to one another, but Lakshmana was particularly close to Rama and followed him like his shadow.

Sixteen blissful years soon flew by. One day, the highly respected Sage Vishvamitra came to the court of King Dashratha. He wanted to take Rama with him to fight the demons who created disturbances in his yajnas.

Dashratha shuddered at the thought of sending his beloved Rama to such danger. But Sage Vashishtha convinced him that Vishvamitra would not let any harm befall Rama. Dashratha could not decline the sage's request. Rama and Lakshmana bowed before their elders, and went with the respected sage.

Vishvamitra taught them some mantras that would help them in time of need. Then they began their difficult journey. After crossing the river Ganga, they reached the Dandaka forest. A she-demon named Tadaka had killed most of the people of the area and now lived here with her two evil sons, Mareecha and Subahu.

The sage said to Rama, "In all the three worlds, you alone can destroy this evil woman. It is your duty to protect the people from evil and sin."

As Rama straightened his bow, the ferocious Tadaka sprang upon him. But Rama's deadly arrow pierced her and she fell lifeless to thc ground.

Rama and Lakshmana, along with Vishvamitra and other sages, proceeded towards Mithila where a contest was to be held for the hand of Sita, the beautiful daughter of King Janaka.

King Janaka had declared that he would marry his daughter to anyone who would bend and string the huge bow given to him by Lord Shiva. None of the kings who had come to try their luck could even move that bow.

Just then, Vishvamitra arrived along with the princes. Now Rama was asked to lift the bow.

Rama lifted the bow with ease and broke it. King Janaka was delighted. The grand royal wedding of Rama and Sita took place among sacred chants in the presence of King Dashratha and King Janaka.

On that joyous occasion, King Janaka married his younger daughter Urmila to Lakshmana. Mandvi and Shrutkirti, the charming daughters of Janaka's younger brother were married to Bharata and Shatrughna respectively, in a grand and regal atmosphere full of golden chariots, music and dance.

The splendour of the wedding defied all descriptions.

The festive party then returned to Ayodhya. The entire city was lavishly decorated to welcome the royal procession. The queens performed arti and welcomed their newly married sons and their brides. They all basked in each other's love and lived happily together.

Rama in Exile

Rama's virtuous and dutiful conduct pleased all. Rama and Sita had been happily married for twelve years. Dashratha was by now old and weak. He thought it was time to coronate Rama as king. Besides being the eldest, he was also the most deserving, with his noble conduct and sense of righteousness.

All his ministers unanimously gave their consent for Rama to be coronated as king. In Dashratha's palace, preparations began amid great joy. Dashratha embraced Rama and said, "Dear son! I have grown old. I wish to coronate you as king tomorrow."

What man plans is not always fulfilled if providence wills othewise.

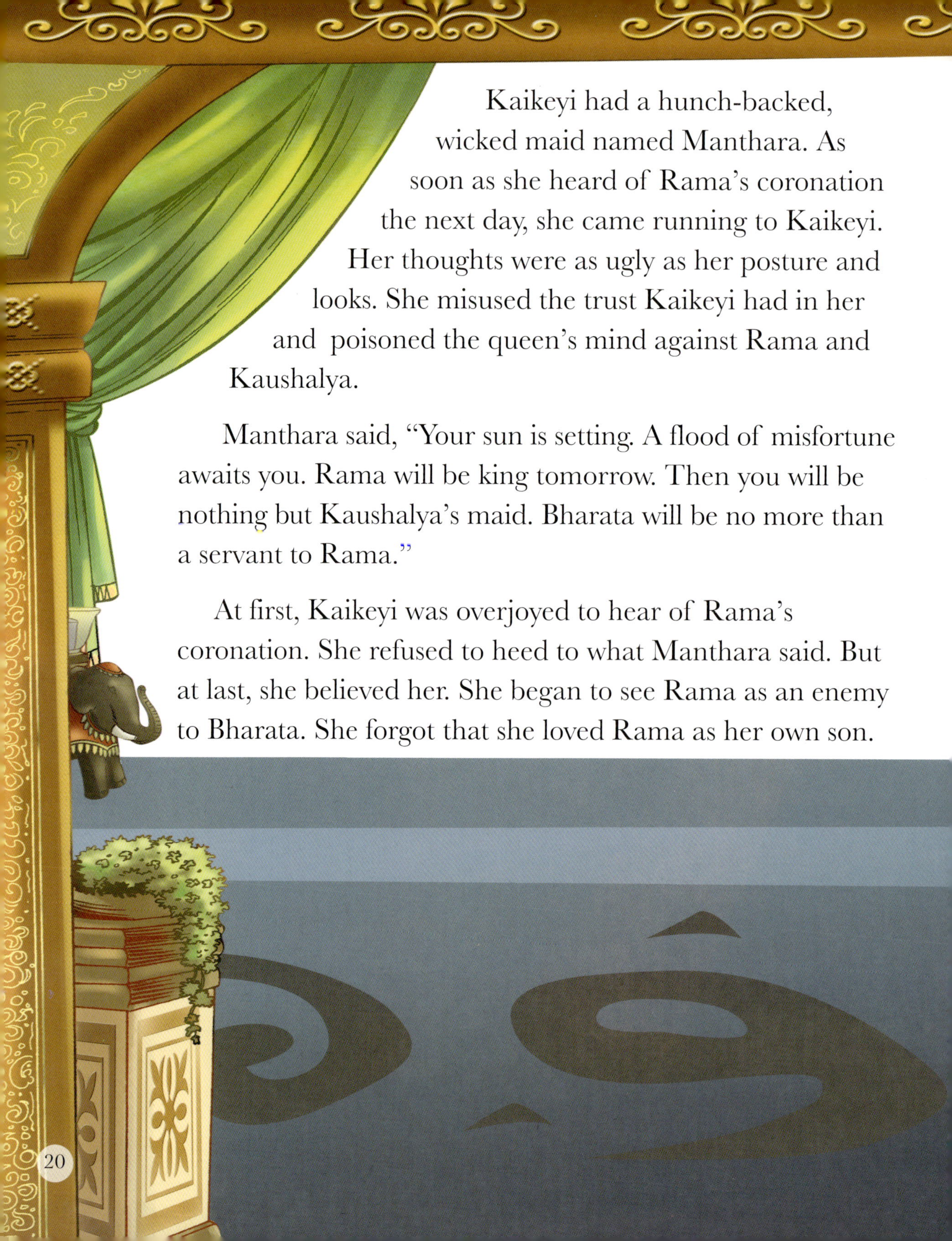

Kaikeyi had a hunch-backed, wicked maid named Manthara. As soon as she heard of Rama's coronation the next day, she came running to Kaikeyi. Her thoughts were as ugly as her posture and looks. She misused the trust Kaikeyi had in her and poisoned the queen's mind against Rama and Kaushalya.

Manthara said, "Your sun is setting. A flood of misfortune awaits you. Rama will be king tomorrow. Then you will be nothing but Kaushalya's maid. Bharata will be no more than a servant to Rama."

At first, Kaikeyi was overjoyed to hear of Rama's coronation. She refused to heed to what Manthara said. But at last, she believed her. She began to see Rama as an enemy to Bharata. She forgot that she loved Rama as her own son.

Kaikeyi then remembered an incident. Once, the wheel of Dashratha's chariot had broken. He would have been killed by the enemy had Kaikeyi not held the wheel with her finger. Dashratha then, had promised to grant her two boons whenever she wanted.

Now was the time to ask for those two boons. She went to the wrath-chamber and lay down on the floor. When Dashratha saw her plight, he lovingly asked her the cause of her misery.

With an evil glint in her eyes, Kaikeyi reminded him of the two boons and said, "Make Bharata the king of Ayodhya and send Rama to exile for fourteen years to Dandaka Vana."

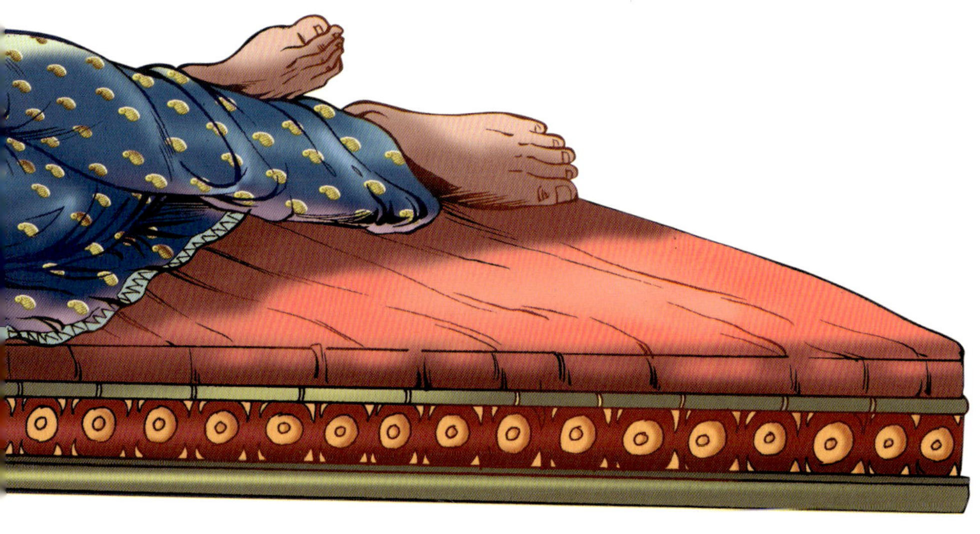

Dashratha fell unconscious on hearing these harsh words. When he came to his senses, he wept and said, "Let Bharata be king but please don't send Rama away from me. I will die without him." But Kaikeyi remained obstinate and hard-hearted. She was blinded by greed and jealousy and summoned Rama to her chamber.

Rama hastened to meet Kaikeyi as soon as he got the message.

message.

Rama was shocked to see Dasharatha in this state of anguish.

On learning of Kaikeyi's desire, Rama said with folded hands, "Mother, what can I do to make my father happy again?" Kaikeyi told him her wish. Noble Rama said, "Mother, I will leave for Dandaka forest this very day. My younger brother Bharata will indeed be a righteous king."

Lakshmana and Sita too, decided to accompany Rama to exile. Rama reminded them of the dangers of the forest. But Sita said, "I am your shadow. I will not be able to live without you. My place is always at your feet."

Dressed as hermits, Rama, Lakshmana and Sita set out for the forest. There was widespread grief in Ayodhya. Weeping and wailing men, women and children followed them, cursing Kaikeyi. The sight was truly heart-rending. Unable to bear the sorrow of Rama's exile, King Dashratha breathed his last.

Bharata and Shatrughna were not there while these events were taking place. They had gone to visit Bharata's maternal uncle Yudhajit, who ruled over the kingdom of Kekaya.

Bharata rushed back when he heard about the cause of Dashratha's death and Rama's exile. He was furious with his mother and swore to bring Rama back. He soon reached Chitrakoot where Rama was at the time. The brothers embraced each other with great affection. Rama was saddened to learn of Dashratha's death.

Bharata pleaded with Rama to return to Ayodhya. But Rama refused saying that he would not break his word of honour, even at the cost of death.

Disappointed and sad, Bharata returned to Ayodhya with Rama's sandals. Placing the sandals on the throne, Bharat began to rule in Rama's name.

Ravana told Mareecha that he wanted to avenge his sister's humiliation. Since Mareecha could transform into any creature he wanted, Ravana asked him to go before Sita in the form of a golden deer.

Mareecha had to obey Ravana's command. He transformed himself into a golden deer and began to graze at the entrance to Rama's hut. Sita expressed to Rama her desire to have the golden deer. Rama at once went after the deer to fulfil his beloved wife's wish.

Before leaving, Rama asked Lakshmana to protect Sita. As Rama's arrow hit the deer, it cried out in Rama's voice, "Oh, Lakshmana!"

Hearing Rama's painful cries, Sita was terrified. She asked Lakshmana to rush immediately to help Rama. Although reluctant to leave Sita alone, Lakshmana drew a line before their cottage. He asked Sita not to step out of it till he returned with Rama.

Ravana was waiting for this moment when he would find Sita alone. He then came to the cottage disguised as a hermit, chanting Vedic hymns, begging for alms. He insisted that Sita step out of the Lakshmana Rekha to give him food. The moment she stepped out, Ravana carried her away in his chariot, up in the sky and flew towards Lanka.

Sita went wailing aloud as the chariot flew through the clouds. Jatayu, the old vulture king, heard her pitiful cries. He came to save Sita. Jatayu fought bravely with his sharp talons and wounded Ravana.

But Ravana cut off his wings and flew away with the wailing Sita. Sita cried, "Oh, Rama! Oh, Lakshmana! Help me!" Sita saw some monkeys sitting in the forest and she threw her jewels down at them.

The Search for Sita

On returning to their hut after killing the golden deer who was the form-changing demon Mareecha, Rama and Lakshmana realised that Sita had been abducted. Griefstricken, they began to search for her. As they went further, they found the wounded Jatayu. "Ravana has carried her away. I fought hard to save her." Saying this, Jatayu, the King of Vultures, breathed his last.

On the way, Rama met Kabandha who advised them to take Sugreeva's help. They also received the hospitality of the pious Shabri who had recognised Vishnu in his Rama Avatar.

As directed by Kabandha, Rama and Lakshmana proceeded towards the Rishyamukha Mountain. The Monkey Chief Sugreeva noticed the two mighty heroes approaching him and felt a sense of dread.

The fact that the two brothers were well-armed, aroused his suspicion that Bali, his elder brother had planned to kill him. Sugreeva was hiding in the Rishyamukha Mountain because Bali could not come there due to a curse on him.

Sugreeva's minister Hanumana was wise and intelligent and could read the motives of other people. He told Sugreeva not to fear. Sugreeva then said to Hanumana, "Disguise yourself as an ordinary being and find out about these two men."

Hanumana left off the mountain and approached the brothers. "You look like kings or royal sages. What brings you here?" he asked politely. He then introduced himself and told them about Sugreeva and his wicked brother Bali.

Lakshmana then proceeded to tell Hanumana all about what had brought them there. Hanumana was thrilled to hear what Lakshmana said.

Hanumana then revealed his original form. He instantly recognised Rama as his Lord and fell at his feet. Hanumana then took the two princes on his shoulders. The three then proceeded to meet Sugreeva.

The route through the mountains was difficult and rough.

Hanumana convinced Sugreeva to make an alliance of friendship with Rama. Sugreeva was pleased with what Hanumana said and his fear of Rama vanished.

Sugreeva spoke warmly to Rama, "It is an honour for me that you seek my friendship. Let us promise to stand by each other." Rama embraced Sugreeva with affection. Promising that he would help Rama get back Sita, Sugreeva said, "I too need your help. My brother Bali has taken away my wife. I am stricken with fear and sorrow." Rama assured him that he would kill Bali. After a fierce battle, Bali was killed by Rama. Sugreeva was happy to get his wife back.

Sugreeva kept his promise to help Rama find Sita. All the monkeys, in the forests, in the seas and lakes, and in the mountains were urged to come forward and join the army to help Rama.

Sugreeva then divided his monkey army into four divisions, and sent them to the four directions with proper instructions as to how to search for Sita.

Sugreeva had great expectation from Hanumana for his speed, valour, wisdom and familiarity with modes of diplomacy and negotiations. Rama too understood Hanumana's unique gifts and realised that he was particularly capable of making their mission a success.

Angad, along with Nala, Hanumana, Jambavan and several others were sent southwards.

Rama gave Hanumana his signet ring with his name engraved on it, so that Sita would recognise him as a messenger from Rama. He said, "Give this ring to Sita and tell her that soon I shall slay Ravana." Hanumana replied, "My Lord, your wish is my command!"

The great Hanumana took the ring and honoured it by touching it to his forehead as a mark of respect. Then he touched Rama's feet and set off on his journey. Rama said, "With your strength and courage, I know that you will find Sita."

Hanumana Finds Sita

Hanumana's army marched southwards and reached the shores of the vast sea. There they met Jatayu's elder brother Sampati who too had seen Ravana carry off Sita towards Lanka.

Hanumana then ascended Mount Mahendra, and with a mighty leap, flew above the waters of the ocean. On the way, he met Surasa the mother of serpents. Surasa tested his strength and blessed him.

Then Hanumana landed on the shores of the island of Lanka which was shimmering like gold.

When night had fallen, Hanumana, who could assume any shape at will, reduced his size and entered the wonderful city. He saw that Ravana's gold palace was guarded by his choicest warriors. It seemed that the city was unassailable even by the gods! *How will I manage to see Sita alone and in secret and remain unnoticed by Ravana?* Hanumana thought in despair..

Hanumana began his search for Sita and reached the Ashoka Vatika. He jumped from one tree to another looking all around. At last, he saw a graceful woman sitting under the Ashoka tree, surrounded by ferocious rakshasis. Tears flowed down her cheeks as she wore a sorrowful look. She was thin and pale from fasting. She sighed deeply again and again, but still she shone like a moonbeam. Hanumana watched her and inferred that this was Sita. He was beside himself with joy at having found her.

At dawn, Hanumana saw the ten-headed Ravana adorned with all his jewels, coming straight towards the Ashoka Vatika. He approached Sita and said, "You have captured my heart. Be my wife and rule over all my other wives. They shall wait on you as apsaras serve the goddesses." Sita began to tremble with rage.

Ravana requested her to bestow her favours on him and to forget Rama. He offered her rich gifts.

The virtuous Sita turned her back on Ravana and said, “I am the chaste and virtuous wife of another man. You cannot tempt me with wealth and power. I belong to Rama just as the rays belong to the Sun. Do the right thing and return me to Rama. O sinner, do not have an evil eye for me. You are doomed to die at Rama’s hands for abducting me.” Ravana was very angry on hearing these words and threatened her in many ways.

Hanumana was pained to see Sita grieving and afraid. He did not know how to console her. He softly began to narrate the story of Rama. Sita was delighted to hear the sweet voice. Then she saw Hanumana sitting atop the tree.

Hanumana prostrated himself before her in reverence and said, "Mother, I am Rama's messenger. Rama will soon attack Lanka and kill Ravana." Then Hanumana gave her the signet ring with Rama's name inscribed on it. Sita's face glowed with joy when she saw the ring. She took it and felt as happy as if she had been reunited with Rama. Sita then pulled out a jewel from her hair and gave it to Hanumana. Give this to Rama and tell him that I do not have more than two months to survive." Hanumana bowed to Sita and prepared to leave.

Hanumana then destroyed Ravana's garden. He uprooted the trees. The animals and snakes were set free. The people of Lanka were terrified by the shrieking of the birds and the crashing of the trees. They ran in all directions.

None of Ravana's demons could capture Hanumana. Hanumana kept growing in size. He kept chanting Rama's name and slaughtered the demons.

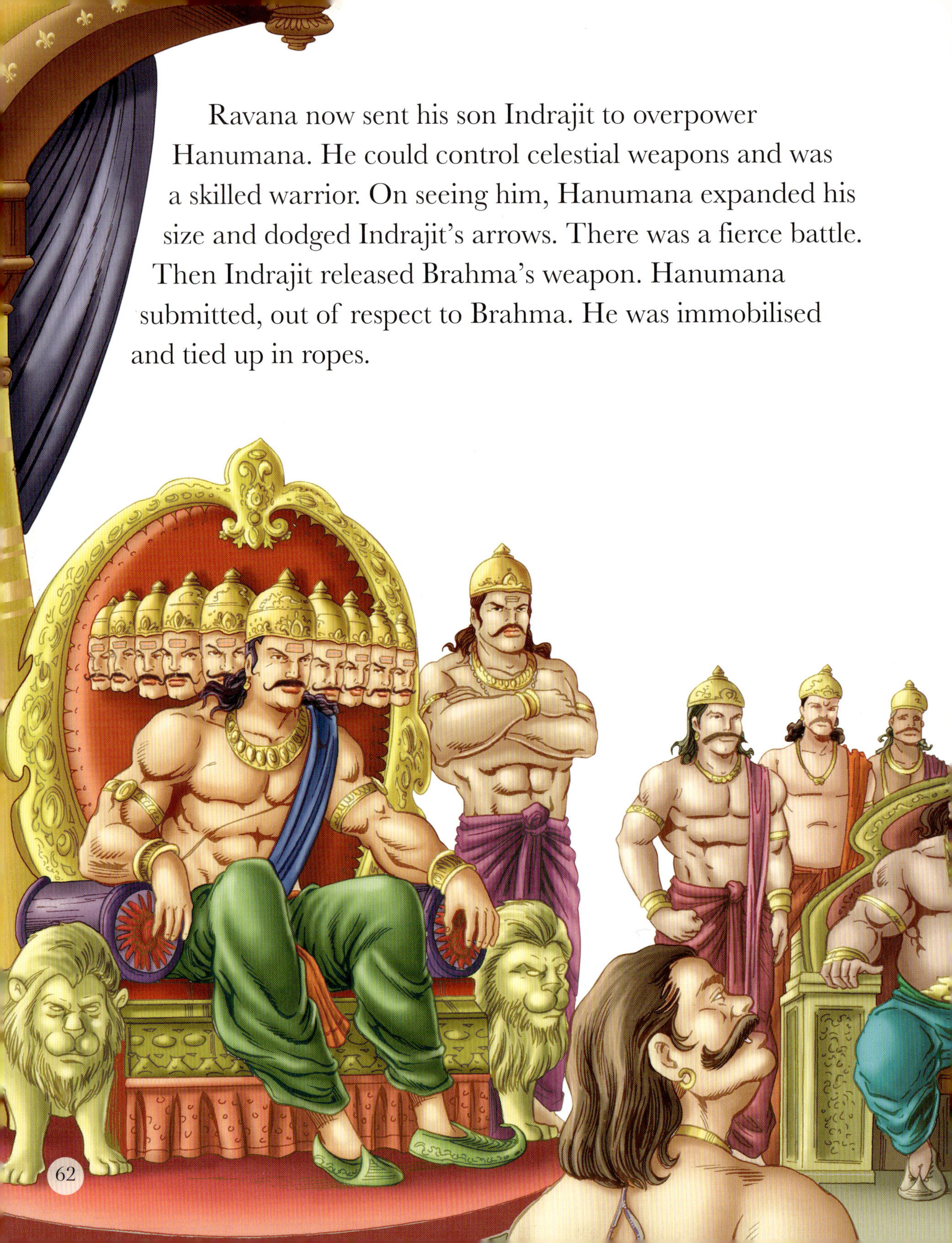

Ravana now sent his son Indrajit to overpower Hanumana. He could control celestial weapons and was a skilled warrior. On seeing him, Hanumana expanded his size and dodged Indrajit's arrows. There was a fierce battle. Then Indrajit released Brahma's weapon. Hanumana submitted, out of respect to Brahma. He was immobilised and tied up in ropes.

Hanumana was dragged to the royal court where Ravana was sitting on his splendid throne. Hanumana introduced himself as the wind-god's son and warned Ravana to return Sita or be prepared to face death.

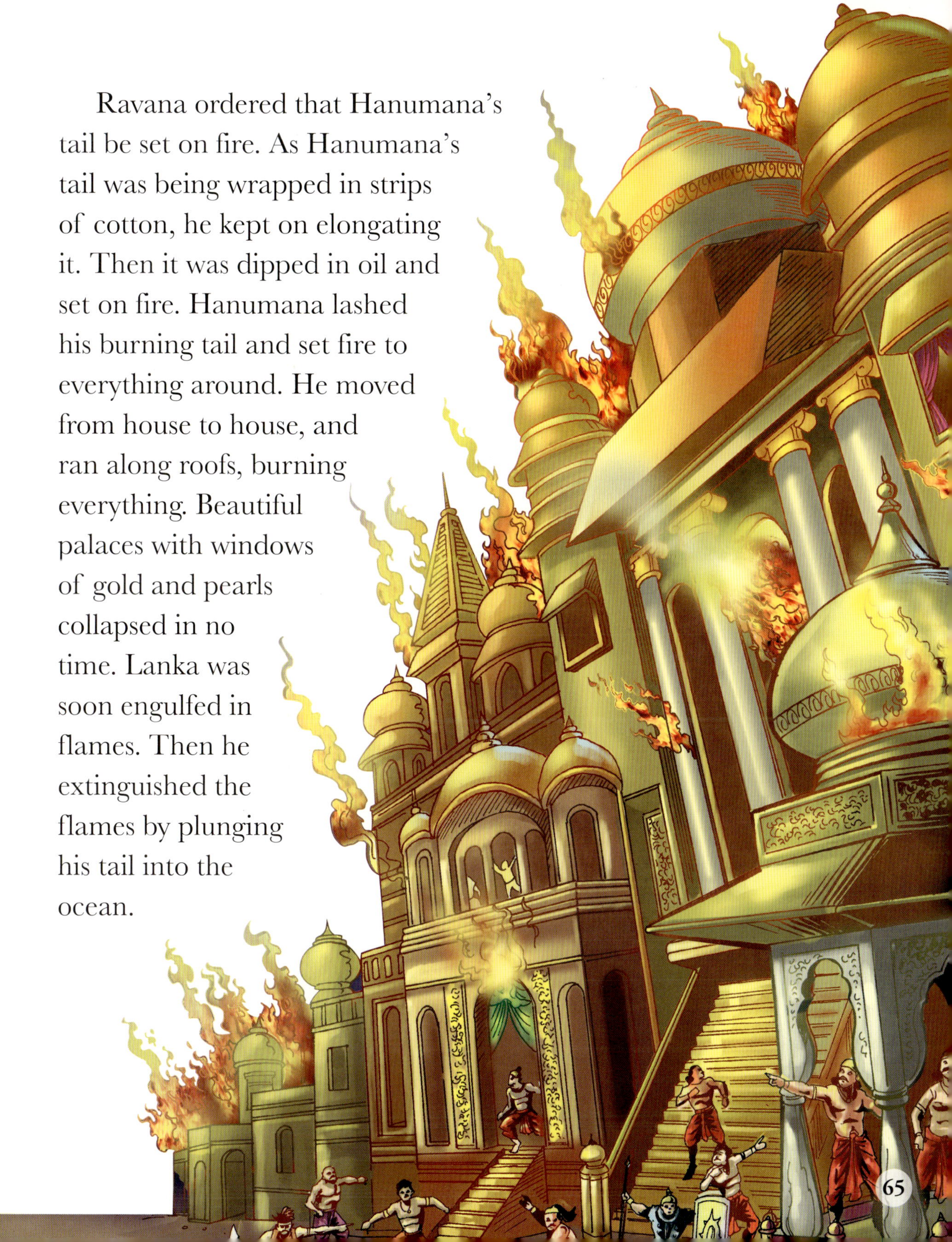

Ravana ordered that Hanumana's tail be set on fire. As Hanumana's tail was being wrapped in strips of cotton, he kept on elongating it. Then it was dipped in oil and set on fire. Hanumana lashed his burning tail and set fire to everything around. He moved from house to house, and ran along roofs, burning everything. Beautiful palaces with windows of gold and pearls collapsed in no time. Lanka was soon engulfed in flames. Then he extinguished the flames by plunging his tail into the ocean.

Spurred on with the thought of seeing Rama again, Hanumana stood atop the mountain and flew over the ocean swiftly to land on Mount Mahendra. The monkeys surrounded him, their faces shining with joy. "I have met Sita," Hanumana announced.

The monkeys were overcome with emotion. Angada, Jambavan and the other monkeys sat down to hear about Hanumana's leap across the ocean, about Lanka and his meeting with Ravana and Sita. Hanumana told them everything from beginning to end.

Then they went to Kishkindha to announce their success to Rama. With great respect, Hanumana told Rama about the trials of Sita, the two-month period that Ravana had given her to live, and her immense faith in Rama.

Rama cried in grief. Soon, with great confidence, Rama vowed to cross the ocean and bring Sita back.

Rama's Victory

In vast numbers, the enthusiastic monkeys and the bears then marched towards the southern ocean. They set out to build a bridge of rocks, trees, and stones. After working for five days and nights, they joyfully crossed over to Lanka.

Ravana's younger brother Vibhishana advised him that it would be best to return Sita to Rama and reconcile. Ravana was very angry and told him that he was a disgrace to their clan.

Humiliated, Vibhishana sought refuge with Rama. Initially, Rama's army eyed him with suspicion, but Rama said, "You should never turn away someone who seeks your friendship." Vibhishana was treated as an equal and taken in as an ally.

The monkey army rushed to Lanka with huge boulders and trees. Rama and Lakshmana killed thousands of rakshasas with their arrows. The rakshasas too fought with spears, maces, clubs and battle axes.The fierce battle between two brave and determined armies littered the ground with wounded or dead monkeys and rakshasas.

Ravana's son Indrajit let loose a shower of arrows which turned into snakes and bound Rama and Lakshmana, so that they could not move. Then a huge bird, Garuda, emerged from the sky and scared away the snakes.

During the fierce battle, Ravana hurled a spear that lodged itself in Lakshmana's chest. Rama was inconsolable. Hanumana quickly flew and got the entire mountain with the Sanjivani herb that cured Lakshmana.

Vibhishana knew that Ravana had the potion of immortality hidden in his navel. He urged Rama to aim his arrow at that spot. As soon as the arrow struck Ravana, he tumbled out of his chariot and fell to the ground.

The gods were delighted with Ravana's death for he had tormented the world for a long time.

The monkeys proclaimed Ravana's death and Rama's victory with glee. The sky resounded with the beating of drums.

Rama told Vibheeshana to give Ravana an appropriate funeral. He was draped with costly clothes. Curd, ghee and roasted gram was sprinkled over him. Vibheeshana lit the pyre with great reverence. After that, Rama crowned Vibheeshana as the king of Lanka.

Rama Returns to Ayodhya

Rama, Sita, Lakshmana, along with Sugreeva, Hanumana and the other monkey warriors returned to Ayodhya which was decorated like a bride. Bharata fell at Rama's feet.

There was much rejoicing all around as Rama was coronated. Lamps were lit in each house.

Henceforth, the festival of Diwali began to be celebrated by the worshippers of Rama with great pomp and enthusiasm.

OTHER TITLES IN THIS SERIES

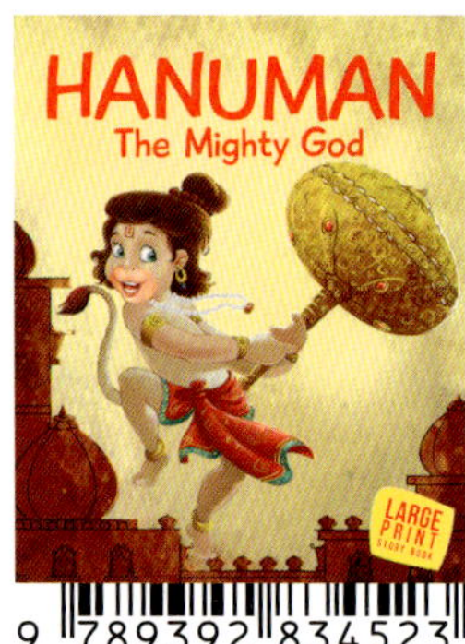

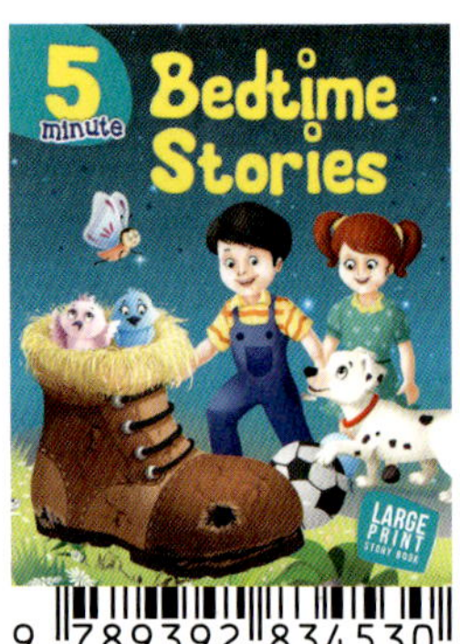

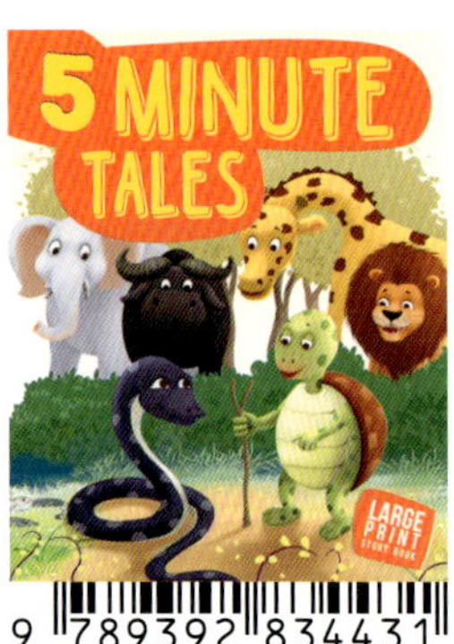

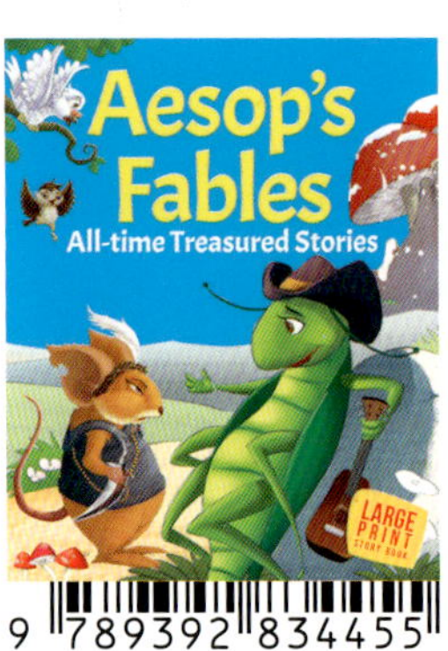

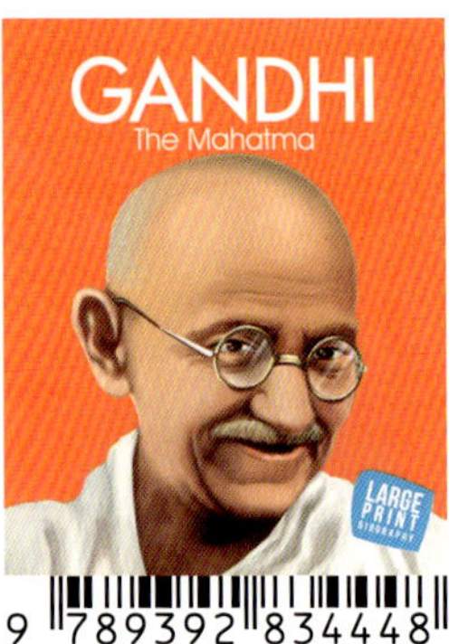